LET GO

by FÉNELON

Whitaker House

Publisher's note:
This edition from Whitaker House has been updated for
the modern reader. Words, expressions, and sentence
structure have been revised for clarity and readability.

Unless otherwise indicated, all Scripture quotations
are taken from the King James Version (KJV)
of the Holy Bible.

LET GO

ISBN-13: 978-0-88368-010-0
ISBN-10: 0-88368-010-6
Printed in the United States of America
© 1973 by Whitaker House

Whitaker House
1030 Hunt Valley Circle
New Kensington, PA 15068
www.whitakerhouse.com

20 21 22 23 24 25 25 **ᴜᴜ** 12 11 10 09 08 07 06

TABLE OF CONTENTS

INTRODUCTION

It was Henry Van Dyke who said, "*Self* is the only prison that can bind the soul." Every Christian who is really serious about living the Christ-like life craves freedom from this bondage. The intensity of the struggle which goes on in the hearts of countless Christians gives testimony to the great need for us to learn to let go of our selfish, sinful lives to become the new creations Jesus meant us to be.

The letters collected in this book were originally penned by François de Salignac de La Mothe Fénelon, the Archbishop of Cambrai, France, during the seventeenth century. While in the office of Archbishop, Fénelon had the opportunity of becoming the spiritual advisor of a small number of earnest people at the Court of Louis the Fourteenth, who sought, under Fénelon's wise direction, to live a life of true spirituality in the midst of a court life which was shamelessly immoral. During his association with these people, he had many opportunities to write, encouraging them to press toward the goal of Christian perfection.

The book should be read in a devotional mood if it is to fulfill its purpose of revealing to the reader the spiritual wisdom, insights and convictions of a truly great spiritual giant. It must be read slowly. The rush and speed of our modern life does not make it easy for us to go at the devotional pace which is "not faster than a walk." We normally skim over newspapers and magazines hurriedly, but in devotional reading our whole being (not only our intellects) must be quieted and made open, receptive and expectant.

Consider turning to this book not primarily to expose your mind to idea, but rather to seek to enter into companionship with this friend of God. Through reading this book we are going to school at the feet of a truly great saint to catch by contagion something of his intimate companionship with God.

These particular letters were previously printed under the title SPIRITUAL LETTERS, a translation by Midred Whitney Stillman. After rereading them, it was decided that a modern paraphrased version would help twentieth century Christians understand the message more clearly. The work passed through the hands of several members of our Editorial Staff before appearing in its present form. We send this message out with the prayer that it will enable more Christians to obtain strength and victory in their lives.

Robert E. Whitaker
President
Whitaker House

LETTER 1

The Advantages of Humility

I often pray to God that He would keep you in the hollow of His hand. And this He certainly will do if you remember to keep a humble and obedient spirit. Humility is good in every situation, because it produces that teachable spirit which makes everything easy. And you, of all people, would be more guilty than many others if you made any resistance to the Lord on this point. For on the one hand, the Lord has taught you so much on the necessity of becoming like a little child; and on the other, few people have had an experience more fitting to humiliate the heart and destroy self-confidence. The good that comes from any experience of personal weakness is the realization that God wants us to be lowly and obedient. So may the Lord keep you!

LETTER 2

How to Bear Suffering Peacefully

Concerning our friend, I pray that God will give him a simplicity of trust that will bring him peace. When we are careful to instantly let go of all needless worries and restless thoughts (that is, self-centered thoughts, rather than loving, outgoing ones), then we shall find ourselves on plateaus of peace even in the midst of the straight and narrow. We shall find ourselves walking in the freedom and innocent peace of the children of God, not lacking wholesome relationships either toward God or man.

I willingly apply to myself the same advice that I give to others, for I am convinced that I must seek my own peace in the same direction. Even now my soul is suffering, but I am aware that it is the life of self which causes us pain; that which is dead does not suffer. If we were really dead, and our life hid with Christ in God (Colossians 3:3), we would no longer struggle with those pains in spirit that now afflict us. So we must learn to bear all sufferings with composure, even those which come upon us through no fault of our own. But we must beware of that restless-

2

ness of spirit which might be our own fault. We can add to our God-given cross by agitated resistance and an unwillingness to suffer. This is simply an evidence of the remaining life of self.

A cross which comes from God ought to be welcomed without any concern for self. And when you accept your cross this way, even though it is painful, you will find that you can bear it in peace. But when you receive your cross unwillingly, you will find it to be doubly severe. The resistance within is harder to bear than the cross itself! But if you recognize the hand of God, and make no opposition to His Will, you will have peace in the midst of affliction. Happy indeed are they who can bear their sufferings with this simple peace and perfect submission to the will of God! Nothing so shortens and soothes suffering as this spirit of non-resistance.

But usually we want to drive a bargain with God. We would at least like to suggest some limits so that we can see an end to our sufferings. We don't realize how we are thwarting the purposes of God when we take this attitude. Because the stubborn clinging to life which makes the cross necessary in the first place, also tends us to reject that cross—at least in part. So we have to go over the same ground again and again.

We end up suffering greatly, but to very little

purpose. May the Lord deliver us from falling into that state of soul in which crosses are of no benefit to us. God loves a cheerful giver, according to St. Paul in Second Corinthians 9:7. Ah! What must be His love for those who, in cheerful and absolute abandonment, give themselves completely to be crucified with Christ!

LETTER 3

The Beauty of the Cross

I am amazed at the power that comes to us through suffering; we are worth nothing without the cross. Of course, I tremble and agonize while it lasts, and all my words about the beneficial effects of suffering vanish under the torture. But when it is all over, I look back on the experience with deep appreciation, and am ashamed that I bore it with so much bitterness. I am learning a great deal from my own foolishness!

So, regardless of the afflictions your friend is bearing, she is blessed in being so quiet under the hand of God. If she dies, she will go *to* the Lord; if she lives she will live *for* Him.

The Kingdom of God began at Calvary. The cross was a necessity. When we pick up the cross of Jesus and bear it in love to Him, his Kingdom has begun in us. We must be satisfied to carry that cross as long as it is His will. You have need of the cross as well as I. The faithful Giver of every good gift distributes them to each of us with His own hand. Blessed be His name! Every cross He gives us is for our profit!

LETTER 4

The Death of Self

I cannot express to you how deeply I sympathize with you in your time of suffering. I suffer right along with you, but still, it cheers me up to know that God loves you.

And the very proof that God loves you is that He does not spare you, but lays upon you the cross of Jesus Christ. Whatever spiritual knowledge or feelings we may have, they are all a delusion if they do not lead us to the real and constant practice of dying to self. And it is true that we do not die without suffering. Nor is it possible to be considered truly dead while there is any part of us which is yet alive. This spiritual death (which is really a blessing in disguise) is undeniably painful. It cuts "swift and deep into our innermost thoughts and desires with all their parts, exposing us for what we really are." The great Physician who sees in us what we cannot see, knows exactly where to place the knife. He cuts away that which we are most reluctant to give up. And how it hurts! But we must remember that pain is only felt where there is life, and where there is life is just the place where death is needed. Our Father wastes no

6

time by cutting into parts which are already dead. Do not misunderstand me; He wants you to live abundantly, but this can only be accomplished by allowing Him to cut into that fleshly part of you which is still stubbornly clinging to life. Don't expect God to deal with those vulgar, wicked desires which you renounced forever when you gave yourself away to him. That part of you is already dead. But, He will deal with the parts of you that are still alive. He might even test your faith with restrictions and trials of all kinds.

Should you resist? Certainly not! You must learn to suffer all things! The death of self must be voluntary, and it can only be accomplished as far as you allow. Anyone who resists death and repels its advances shows that he is not willing to die. You must be willing to yield to the will of God whenever He decides to remove from you all of the props on which you have leaned. Sometimes you must give up even your most spiritual friends, if they are props. "What fearest thou, oh thou of little faith?"

Do you fear that He may not be able to supply to you from Himself that help which He may have taken away on the human level? And why does He take human help away, except to supply you from Himself, and to purify you by the painful lesson?

I know how confined you are, but I am convinced that God means to accomplish His work in you by cutting off every human resource. He is a jealous God, and He wants you to understand that what He is about to perform in you has been done by Himself alone, and by no other.

So give yourself up to His plans. Allow yourself to be led wherever He wants to lead you. And be careful to not seek help from your friends if God is forbidding it. Your friends can only give you what He gives them for you. Why be so concerned about the dried-up streams when the rivers of living water are so available?

LETTER 5

Peace Comes Through Simplicity and Obedience

Learn to cultivate peace. And you can do this by learning to turn a deaf ear to your own ambitious thoughts. Or haven't you yet learned that the strivings of the human mind not only impair the health of your body, but also bring dryness to the soul. You can actually consume yourself by too much inner striving. And to no purpose at all! Your peace and inner sweetness can be destroyed by a restless mind. Do you think that God can speak in those soft tender accents that melt the soul, in the midst of such inner confusion as you permit by that endless, hurrying parade of thoughts going through your mind? Be quiet, and He will soon be heard. The only principle you need to be concerned about is to be scrupulously obedient.

You have been asking for comfort and peace. But you do not understand that you have been led to the brink of the fountain, and are refusing to drink. Peace and comfort can be found no-where except in simple obedience. So be faithful in obeying even when you do not understand, and you will soon find that the rivers of living

9

water will flow, as God has promised. You will receive according to the measure of your faith: much, if you believe much; nothing, if you believe nothing and continue to listen to your own restless thoughts.

You dishonor the meaning of Christian love when you suppose that a man who truly loves God could ever be worried about these trifles which are continually clamoring for your attention. Christian love goes straight to God in pure simplicity, knowing that these trifles are no problem to Him. Satan is the one who torments us with trivialities. And he often transforms himself into an angel of light, and bothers us with endless self-examinations and an over-sensitive conscience which allows us no peace. I'm sure you know by experience the trouble and spiritual danger which Satan can bring upon you in this way. But you can be victorious. Everything depends upon your faithfulness in repelling his first advances.

If you will learn to be honest and simple in your desires, I think you will be more pleasing to God than if you were to suffer a hundred martyrdoms. If there is anything you should be concerned about, it is simply your own hesitation in offering a sacrifice so right in the sight of God. Can true love hesitate when it is required to please its Well-beloved?

LETTER 6

The True Source of Peace Is in the Surrender of the Will

Live in continued peace. But understand that peace does not depend upon the fervor of your devotion. The only thing you need to be concerned about is the direction of your will.

Give that up to God without reservation. The important question is not how religious you are, or how devoted, but rather is your will in harmony with God's? Humbly confess your faults. Learn to be detached from the world and completely abandoned to God. Love Him more than yourself and His glory more than your life. The least you can do is to desire and ask for such a love. God will then pour out upon you that special love which only His children know, and He will give you His peace.

LETTER 7

True Goodness Is Only Reached by Abandonment

Evil circumstances are changed into good when they are received with an enduring trust in the love of God, while good circumstances may be changed into evil when we become attached to them through the love of self. Nothing in us or around us is truly good until we become detached from the world and totally abandoned to God. So, even though you are now in these bad circumstances, put yourself confidently and without reserve into His hand. I would give anything to see you in better circumstances. But if evil circumstances have taught you to be sick of the love of the world, then that is good. That love of self, which the world advocates, is a thousand times more dangerous than any poison. I pray for you with all my heart.

LETTER 8

"Knowledge Puffeth Up; Charity Edifyeth"

I was happy to receive your letter, and to find you sharing with me so simply and openly everything that has been taking place within your spirit. Never hesitate to write me whatever you think God wants you to write.

It is not at all surprising that you have a strong ambition to move ahead in spiritual things, and to be closely acquainted with well-known Christians. It is very flattering to self when it can gain some esteem by being very religious, and it eagerly seeks such esteem. Oh, how careful we need to be about our motives! The progress we are making in the Christian life and the celebrated Christian friends we are making may be all wrongly motivated if we are simply gratifying self. Our aim should be to die to the flattering delights of self-love. Our aim should be, not greatness, but humility. We must learn to love personal obscurity and contempt, so that our only concern is to glorify God.

We can listen to endless sermons about Christian growth, and become perfectly familiar

13

with the language, and yet be as far from its attainment as ever. Our great aim should be to be deaf to self, to listen quietly to God, to renounce every bit of pride and to devote ourselves to living. Let's learn to talk less and do more without caring whether anyone sees us or not.

God can teach more than even the most experienced Christians know. He can teach you better than all the books that the world has ever seen. But be careful about your motives in this eager chase after knowledge. You are aware, aren't you, that all we need is to be poor in spirit, and to know nothing but Christ and Him crucified. Although being a know-it-all makes us feel important, what is really needed to strengthen Christian character is love. So don't be satisfied with anything less than love. You certainly don't think it possible that the love of God and the dethroning of self can only be reached through the acquisition of knowledge. You already have more knowledge than you can use. You would do better to put into practice what you already know. Oh how we deceive ourselves when we suppose that we are growing in grace because our vain curiosity is being gratified by the enlightenment of our intellect! We need to be humble, and understand that we cannot receive God's gifts from man. The love of God comes to us only from Jesus.

LETTER 9

We Are Not to Choose the Manner in Which Our Blessings Shall Be Bestowed

I think you know what God requires of you. The question is, will you do it? You understand that your love of self is causing the struggle you are having with the will of God. So now what you must decide is this: are you going to allow pride and selfish ambitions to keep you from doing what God in His mercy wants you to do? You are so careful about passing thoughts which bob into your mind and out again, and worry about so many details that you should not be thinking about. Why are you not as careful about your continued resistance to the Holy Spirit? Is this continued resistance due to the fact that He has not given you what you want in a way that will flatter your ego?

What does it matter if you receive the gifts of grace as beggars receive bread? The gifts themselves are no less pure nor precious. God loves this beggar-like humility, and delights to send help to such people. Isn't this the way you put off self by humbling yourself before God and

15

confessing yourself helpless without Him? Isn't humility an instrument of God which makes us have faith in Him rather than ourselves? Isn't this the way that you die to the life of self within? And if not, then what do you expect to accomplish by all your reading about pure love and your frequent devotions? How can you read what condemns the very depths of your soul? You need to understand that you are being influenced by selfish pride when you reject the gifts of God, just because they do not come in a shape that suits your taste. It is difficult for me to understand how you can pray when you have an attitude like this. What is God telling you in the depths of your soul? He asks nothing but death, and you desire nothing but life. How can you send up to Him a prayer for His grace, with a restriction that He shall send it only by a channel demanding no sacrifice on your part? Can you expect God to minister to the gratification of selfish pride?

LETTER 10

The Discovery and Death of Self

Yes, I am happy to have you call me your father! Because I certainly am—and always will be. You only need more assurance that I love you as a father, and this assurance will come when your heart is freed from the bondage of selfish love. We are in confining quarters, indeed, when we are enclosed in self, but when we emerge from that prison, and enter into the immensity of God and the liberty of His children, we are truly free.

Though it sounds strange to say it I am rejoicing that God has reduced you to a state of weakness. Your ego can neither be convinced nor forced into submission by any other means: it is always finding secret lines of supply from your own courage; it is always discovering impenetrable retreats in your own cleverness. It was hidden from your eyes while it fed upon the subtle poison of an apparent generosity as you constantly sacrificed yourself for others. But now God has forced it to cry aloud, to come forth into open day and display its excessive jealousy. Oh, how painful, but how beneficial these times of weakness! As long as any self-love is remaining, we are always

17

afraid it will be revealed. But God does not give up as long as the least symptom of it lurks in the innermost recesses of the heart, God pursues it. and by some infinitely merciful blow, forces it into the open. And the sight of the problem then becomes the cure. Self-love, forced into the light, sees itself as it really is in all its deformity and despair and disgrace. And in a moment, the flattering illusions of your whole selfish life are dissipated. God sets before your eyes your idol: self. You look at that spectacle and you cannot turn your eyes away. Nor can you hide the sight from others.

To expose self-love in this way without its mask is the most mortifying punishment that can ever be inflicted. We no longer see self as wise, prudent, polite, composed, and courageous in sacrificing itself for others. It is no longer the old self-love whose diet consisted in the belief that it had need of nothing, and deserved everything. It weeps from the rage that it has wept. It cannot be stilled, and refuses all comfort, because its poisonous character has been detected. It sees itself foolish, rude, and impudent, and is forced to look its own frightful countenance in the face. It says with Job, "For the thing I greatly feared is come upon me, and that which I was afraid of is come unto me" (Job 3:25). For it is that which it fears most that will be its destruction.

We have no need that God should attack in us that which is lifeless and unresponsive. (It is the living only that must die). Nothing else matters. So you see why I rejoice in your state of weakness. This is what you needed—to behold a self-love defeated, sensitive, impure, and exposed for what it really is. And now all you have to do is to quietly look at it as it is. The moment you can do this, self will disappear.

You asked for a remedy, that your problems might be cured. You do not need to be cured. you need to be slain. Quit looking for a remedy and let death come. This is the only way to deal with self. Be careful however of that bitter bravery that decides to accept no remedy, for this itself may become a remedy in disguise, giving a type of satisfaction and comfort to your ego. Do not seek any comfort from self-love, and do not conceal the disease. Uncover everything in simplicity and holiness and then allow yourself to die.

But understand that this is not done by any exertion of your own strength. When you finally see self for what it is, weakness has become your only possession. Strength is not even in the picture. And if you had any, it would only make the agony longer and more distressing. If you die from weakness and weariness, you will die more quickly and less violently. A dying life must of necessity be painful. Kindnesses are a cruelty to one who is being tortured to death. All he longs for is that one fatal blow—not food, not sustenance. In fact, if it were possible to weaken him even further and hasten his death, we would be shortening his sufferings. But we can do nothing. Only the hand that tied him down to that place of torture can deliver that fatal blow that will set him free.

So do not ask for either remedies or sustenance. Do not even ask for death. To ask death is impatience. And to ask food or remedies is only to prolong the agony. What, then, shall we do? Do nothing. Seek to nothing. Hold to nothing. Simply confess everything, not as a means of getting relief, but because of humble desire to yield unto Jesus.

Though I am your Father in the Lord, do not look to me as a source of life. I would rather have you consider me as a means of death to your love of self. For just as surgical instruments would fail in fulfilling their purpose if they did not minister to life, so an instrument of death would be falsely named if, instead of slaying, it kept alive. For the time being, I would be that instrument of death. If I seem to be hard, unfeeling, indifferent, pitiless, wearied, annoyed, and contemptuous, God knows how far it is from the truth. But He permits me to seem this way. And I shall be much more serviceable to you in this false and imaginary character than were I to show my real feelings and very human desire to help. You see, the point is not how you are to be sustained and kept alive, but how you are to give up and die.

LETTER 11

The Sight of Our Imperfections Should Not Take Away Our Peace

There is something about your suffering which is very subtle and perhaps hard for you to understand. For even though you are convinced that your first concern is the glory of God, yet in your inmost soul it is the old self which keeps causing you so much trouble. The way I see the problem is this: I think that you really do want God to be glorified in your life, but you think that this is going to be accomplished by becoming more and more perfect. And in doing this you still are thinking of your own personal worth. So if you would truly derive profit from the discovery of your imperfections, I would suggest two things. First of all, never try to justify yourself before God. And second, do not condemn yourself. Instead, why not quietly lay your imperfections before God? And if, at that moment, there are some things you cannot understand about His will, simply tell Him that you are willing to conform your will to His in all things. And then go on in peace. For you must understand that peace is the will of God for you in every situation. There is, in fact, a peace of conscience which non-believers themselves should experience when awakened to repentance by God. And every tear of repentance should be peaceful and equalled with comfort. Remember the beautiful word which once delighted you, that the Lord was not in noise and confusion, but in the still, small voice. (I Kings 19:11-12).

LETTER 12

Living by the Cross and by Faith

We have crosses to bear everyday. But I have learned to enjoy the bitterest of them. And it is sweet to know that the heaviest cross can be borne in peace. However, there may be times when it seems that you do not have the strength even to bear it or to drag it. All you can do is fall down beneath it, overwhelmed and exhausted. I pray that God may spare you as much as possible in proportioning your suffering, not that God delights in seeing us suffer, but He knows that we need this as much as we need our daily bread. And only God knows how much we need to accomplish His purposes in our lives. So what we must do is live by faith and live by the cross. For we are confident that God, with His true compassion, proportions our trials to the amount of strength that He has committed to us within. Even though we cannot actually see this happening, yet we believe it is true. Trial and strength are portioned out in equal measures. Living by this kind of faith demands the deepest kind of death to self.

LETTER 13

Despair at Our Imperfections Is a Greater Obstacle Than the Imperfection Itself

Do not be overly concerned about your defects. Instead concentrate on having an unceasing love for Jesus, and you shall be much forgiven, because you have loved much. (Luke 7:47). However, we need to beware of the tendency to seek the good feelings and selfish thrills of love (which are the by-products of love) instead of love itself. We can so easily deceive ourselves on this matter. We can concentrate so much on love that we miss the point entirely. You are more occupied with the love, says St. Francis of Sales, than with the Well-beloved. If Jesus were the sole object of our love, we would be all wrapped up in Him. But when we are concerned with constant assurance of His love, we are still in a measure busy with self.

When we look at our defects in peace through the spirit of Jesus, they vanish before the majesty of His love. But when we concentrate on our defects, forgetting that Jesus loves us, we become restless, the presence of God is interrupted, and the flow of God's love is hindered. The humilia-

25

tion we feel about our own defects can often be a greater fault than the original defect itself if it keeps you from moving into the realization of God's love. So don't let yourself get taken up with the lesser of the two. Do not be like a person I just met a short time ago, who, after reading the life of one of the saints, was so angry about his own life in comparison that he completely gave up the idea of living a devoted Christian life. I know this will not be true of you.

When I receive your letters, I can just about tell how faithfully you have lived by the amount of peace and freedom you manifest in your writing. The more peaceful and free you are, the nearer you seem to be to God.

LETTER 14

Pure Faith Sees God Alone

Do not worry about the future. It makes no sense to worry if God loves you and has taken care of you. However, when God blesses you remember to keep your eyes on Him and not the blessing. Enjoy your blessings day by day just as the Israelites enjoyed their manna, but do not try to store the blessings for the future. There are two peculiar characteristics of pure faith. It sees God behind all the blessings and imperfect works which tend to conceal Him,* and it holds the soul in a state of continued suspense. Faith seems to keep us constantly up in the air, never quite certain of what is going to happen in the future; never quite

---

* "The man that looks on glass,
 On it may stay his eye;
 Of, if he pleaseth, through it pass,
 And then the heavens espy." — Herbert

   Pure faith does not see the neighbor who succeeds in hurting us nor the disease that attacks our bodies. That would be equivalent to the quote staying its eye upon the glass. And when you look at the glass, you will see a thousand flaws and imperfections that will annoy you. But faith does not look at the glass, it looks through it and discovers God, and what God permits faith can joyfully accept. — Editor

able to touch a foot to solid ground. But faith is willing to let God act with the most perfect freedom, knowing that we belong to Him and are to be concerned only about being faithful in that which he has given us to do for the moment. This moment by moment dependence, this dark, unseeing peacefulness of the soul under the utter uncertainty of the future, is a true martyrdom which takes place silently and without any stir. It is God's way of bringing a slow death to self. And the end comes so imperceptibly that it is often almost as much hidden from the sufferer himself, as from those who don't even know he suffers.

Sometimes in this life of faith God will remove His blessings from you. But remember that He knows how and when to replace them, either through the ministry of others or by Himself. He can raise up children from the very stones.

Eat then your daily bread without worrying about tomorrow. There is time enough tomorrow to think about the things tomorrow will bring. The same God who feeds you today is the very God who will feed you tomorrow. God will see to it that manna falls again from Heaven in the midst of the desert, before His children lack any good thing.

LETTER 15

Our Knowledge Stands in the Way of Our Becoming Wise

Live in quiet peace, my dear young lady, without any thought for the future. For only God knows if you have a future in this world. Perhaps not. In fact, you do not even have a today that you can call your own. A Christian must live out the hours of today in accord with the plans of God, to whom the day truly belongs.

Keep on with the good things you are doing, since you feel a leaning in these directions, and certainly you will be able to get them done. But be careful of distractions and the desire to do too many things at once. Above all things, be faithful to the present moment, doing one thing at a time, and you will receive all the grace you need.

I am sure that you understand that it is not enough to be merely separated from the world. For we can be separated and be quite proud about it. So we need to give considerable attention to becoming lowly. And I want you to see clearly the distinction between these two things. In separation, we renounce the outer things of the world. But when we turn to the subject of lowliness and

29

humility we are then dealing with the inner self. Every shadow of pride must be left behind. You cannot imagine how dangerous pride is — especially if it is that pride of wisdom and morality which seems so right and kind.

We must take a humble position in every situation. We must never brag about ourselves, and especially not of our goodness or special strength. I have said this because I think you are depending too much on your own strength, your own selflessness, and your own uprightness. What you need to see is that these things are not your own. They are God's.

We can learn a lesson from babies. Babies own nothing. They treat diamonds and apples alike. Be a babe. Have nothing of your own. (It all belongs to God anyway!) Forget yourself. Give way on all occasions. Let the smallest be greater than you.

When you pray, let your prayers be simple loving prayers out of the heart. This is far better than more refined prayers which come only from the head.

You will learn most in times of deprivation, deep meditation and silence of the soul before God. It is here where you will learn to renounce your own selfish spirit and to love humility, obscurity, weakness and submission. These things, so despised by the world, are the accomplished teachers of all truths. Human knowledge can only stand in the way.

LETTER 16

Those Who Injure Us Are to Be Loved and Welcomed as the Hand of God

I certainly sympathize with you in all of your troubles, but I can do nothing else for you except pray that God will comfort you. You have great need of the power of the Holy Spirit, both to sustain you in this time of trouble, and also to restrain you in your natural desire to find a way out.

As to the letter regarding your family background, I think you should lay this matter before God alone, and ask Him to be merciful to the one who wants to hurt you. I have always noticed, or thought that I noticed, that you were quite sensitive on that point. But remember that when God deals with the problem of self, he always attacks the problem where the weakness is. Anyone knows that if you want to kill another person, you do not begin by striking a blow at their hair or their fingernails. No, you direct your attack to the vital organs such as the heart or the brain. Now when God is attacking the problem of self in us, he always touches the tenderest spot, that

32

which is fullest of life. And many of the crosses which God distributes are designed to lay right on the most sensitive areas of our self life. Even though this is a most humiliating experience to go through, it is best for you to allow yourself to be humbled. Quietness and peace during humiliation are the manifestations of Jesus in the soul.

I would also warn you of the temptation of "humble talk." It is so easy to talk in very humble ways simply because it sounds good. But it is far better to be humble and say nothing about it. The humility that can still talk needs to be carefully watched! The old self gets a lot of comfort out of what it says to itself.

Don't allow yourself to be upset by what people are saying about you. Let the world talk. All you need to be concerned about is doing the will of God. As for what people want, you can't please everybody, and it isn't worth the effort. One quiet moment in the presence of God will more than repay you for every bit of slander that will ever be leveled against you. You must learn to love other people without expecting any friendship from them at all. People tend to be quite fickle. They love us and leave us, they go and come. They shift from one position to another like a kite in the wind, or like a feather in the breeze. Let them do as they will. Just be sure that you see only God in them. They could do nothing to you without His permission. So, in the end, it is He that tests or blesses us, using them as we have need.

LETTER 17

Quietness in God Our True Resource

When it comes to accomplishing things for God, you will find that high aspirations, enthusiastic feelings, careful planning and being able to express yourself well are not worth very much. The important thing is absolute surrender to God. You can do anything He wants you to do if you are walking in the light of full surrender.

Living in this blessed way involves a continual death which is known to very few, but it is in this position that you can be really effective for God. A single word spoken to another person from this restful, abandoned position will do more to change circumstances than all our most eager and carefully planned schemes. You see, when you speak from this position of abandonment to God, it is the Spirit of God who is then speaking, and the word you speak out of context loses none of its force and authority. Only one word perhaps— but it enlightens, persuades, blesses, and moves to action. We have accomplished everything, and have scarcely said anything. On the other hand, if the old self gets the way, we end up talking forever. We discuss a thousand different possibilities. We are constantly afraid of not saying or doing enough. We get angry, excited, exhausted, distracted, and finally make no headway at all.

I am saying this because I have noticed a tendency in you to talk about problems rather than abandoning yourself to God and leaving them with Him. And you will be better off both physically and spiritually when you quietly place everything in God's hands.

As the saying goes, "Let the water flow beneath the bridge." You can't change men from being men. People will always be weak, vain, unreliable, unfair, hypocritical and arrogant. The world will always be worldly. And you cannot change it. People will follow their own inclinations and habits. And since you cannot recast their personalities, the best course of action is to let them be what they are and bear with them. Do not allow yourself to be troubled and perplexed when you see people being unreasonable and unjust. Rest in peace in the bosom of God. He sees it all more clearly than you do, and yet He permits it. So be content to do whatever you feel you should, quietly and gently and don't worry about anything else.

LETTER 18

True Friendships Are Founded Only in God

We must be content with the friends that God gives us, without having selfish choices of our own. It is right that His will shall be done, not ours. Better still, His will shall *become* ours without the least reservation, in order that it may be done on earth as it is done in Heaven. This is far more important than satisfying self. Oh, how precious our friendships are, and how near we are to each other when we are all one in Jesus! What heavenly fellowship and conversation is ours when we are thinking only of Him and His will for us. So if you want to find your true friends, I will tell you where to look. Begin with God. He is the only source of true and eternal friendship. You are best suited for spiritual communication and friendship when you sink in silence into the bosom of God. He means everything to the kind of friends you seek. They talk of Him and live for Him and their whole lives are wrapped up in Him. That is why I tell you to sink into His bosom. This is where true friendship is. No matter what means of fellowship you have, you will find them

37

all supplied in the bosom of God. Even if such friends should fail you, you will still be able to confide in God.

LETTER 19

The Cross a Source of Our Pleasure

I sympathize with you in all your heartaches. But I know you understand that we must carry the cross with Christ during this fleeting life. Soon time will give way to eternity and our suffering will be over. Soon God will wipe away our tears with His own hand, and pain and sighing will forever flee away, and we shall reign with Christ. But while this fleeting moment of trial with Christ is permitted us, let us not lose sight of the glory of the cross. If we must suffer, then let us do it quietly and humbly. It is self which is always exaggerating our troubles and making us think that they are bigger than they are. But pay no attention to the complaints of self. A cross carried in simplicity, without the interference of self adding to the weight of it, is not really so bad. If we suffer for Jesus because we love Him, we are not only happy in spite of the cross, but because of it. For love rejoices at the privilege of suffering for the Well-beloved, and the cross which forms us into His image is a comforting bond of love.

LETTER 20

Do Not Be Distressed by the Revelation of Self or the Absence of Feeling

I pray God that this New Year may be full of grace and blessing for you. I am not surprised to hear that you no longer enjoy reminiscing and meditation like you did when you were first recovering in your time of suffering. Everything changes. People of lively dispositions, accustomed to much activity, soon languish away into solitude and inactivity. (And that was your experience, wasn't it?) And in fact, it was this very active disposition of yours which made me so concerned about how you would react to being confined and reduced to a life of quietness. Back in those "good old days," nothing seemed impossible to you. You said with Peter, "It is good for us to be here!" But it is often with us as it was with him. We say this because we don't know what we are talking about! (Mark 9:5-6) In our moments of enjoyment we feel as if we could do anything. And in times of temptation and discouragement, we think we can do nothing. And both ideas are wrong.

But now that you are getting back to your

former self, you should not feel disturbed if it is getting more difficult for you to meditate. I think the cause of this lay concealed within you even when you were suffering and became so zealous about meditation. You are just naturally a very active and eager person. And it was only your weariness and exhaustion that made you long for a life of quietness. But now that things are getting back to normal, do not fear that you are losing the ground you gained during your suffering. For, by being faithful to God, the selfless life of abandonment which He revealed to you will gradually become a permanent part of your more active life. You had only a taste of it during your suffering. Now it will become a principle by which to live. God gave you that experience that you might see where He was leading you. Now He takes away the vividness of that experience that you might be made aware that even the experience does not belong to you. You must see that you are not able, in yourself, either to obtain or keep such an experience. It is a gift of grace that must be asked for in all humility.

So do not be surprised at again finding yourself becoming sensitive, impatient, haughty, and self-willed. You must be made to understand that this is your natural disposition, and without God's grace, you will never be anything different. "We must bear the yoke of the daily confusion of our sins," says St. Augustine. We must be made to feel our weakness, our wretchedness, our inability to correct ourselves. We must give up hope in ourselves, and have no hope but in God. Yet we must bear with ourselves, never flattering ourselves, but never neglecting a single opportunity to correct ourselves.

We need to understand what kind of people we really are while waiting for God to change us. We need to become humble under His all-powerful hand. We need to become submissive and manageable as soon as we sense any resistance in our will. Be silent as much as you can. Be in no hurry to judge, but think through your decisions, your likes and dislikes. In your daily living, stop at once when you are aware that you are getting in too much of a hurry. And do not be too eager even for good things. Take your time.

LETTER 21

The Imperfection of Others to Be Born in Love

It has been a long time since I've written to you, but let me assure you that I am just as attached to you through our Lord as I ever was. In fact, I am more attached now. And I want with all my heart for you to have that same peace and joy in your home which you enjoyed at the beginning. It should be remembered that even the best of people leave much to be desired, and we must not expect too much. We need to be very patient with the faults of others. The most perfect people in the world have many imperfections, and so do we. And sometimes it is quite difficult for us to tolerate each other. We are to "bear one another's burdens, and so fulfill the law of Christ" (Gal. 6:2), and I think this means, among other things, that we are to bear the burden of each others imperfections. Peaceful and harmonious relationships can be helped a great deal if people just learn to be quiet, to be prayerful, and to keep surrendered to the Lord. We must refuse to indulge in criticism and jealous feelings, which make us so hard to live with. We would certainly

43

avoid a lot of trouble if we would just live in this simple way! Happy is the one who pays no attention to his own hasty judgements nor to the gossip of others!

Be content with leading a simple life. Be obedient, and bear your daily cross. You need it, and it is given to you by the mercy of God, for He knows how much you need discipline. You must learn to despise the selfishness of your own heart, and you must also be willing to be despised by others, if God permits it. Learn to draw your strength and nourishment from Jesus, and from Him alone. St. Augustine says that his mother lived on prayer. I would like for you to do the same. Die to everything else. There is no other way to live this Christian life than by a continual death to self.

LETTER 22

The Fear of Death Is Not Taken Away by Our Own Courage But by the Grace of God

I am not surprised in the least to hear that you are thinking about death more and more these days. I guess that's quite natural as we get older and weaker! At least, this is my experience. We reach a point in life in which we are forced to think about the inevitable end which is approaching, and the older and more inactive we become the more we find ourselves dwelling on this matter. We might wish that we could put these thoughts out of our minds, but I remind you that God makes use of these thoughts to keep us from being deceived about how brave we are in the face of death. It is good to think seriously about death so that we are kept aware of our human weaknesses, and kept humble in His hands.

Nothing humbles us more effectively than troubled thoughts about death. And in the midst of such meditations, we often find ourselves wondering whatever happened to all the faith and assurance we thought we had. But this experience is good for us. This is the crucible of humiliation, in which our faith is ground down and tested, in which we see again our own weaknesses and unworthiness, and come to understand afresh our need of God's continuous mercy. In His sight shall no man living be justified (Psalm 143:2). Yea, the heavens are not clean in his sight, (Job 15:15), and in many things we offend all (James 3:2). We see our faults and not our virtues. And this is as it should be, for it is very dangerous to look at our virtues, lest we be deceived into thinking that we do not need God's mercy.

When we come to these valley experiences when we are deprived of faith and assurance, there is only one thing to do. We must go straight on through the valley, walking with the Shepherd just as we did before we entered that valley. As we go through, let us deal with any sin which the Lord reveals to us, still walking in the light He gives. On the other hand, beware of becoming overly sensitive just because you are thinking of death. The Lord does not want you to be concerned about things which do not really matter. We must remain peaceful, not pitying ourselves because death is approaching. Instead, let's keep a detached attitude about life, giving it in sacrifice to God, and keeping ourselves confidently abandoned to Him. When he was dying, St. Ambrose was asked whether he was not afraid to face God at the judgement. He replied with these unforgettable words, "We have a good Master." We need to remind ourselves of this.

There is much uncertainty about death, even for the Christian. We are not exactly certain how God is going to judge us, nor can we be absolutely sure about our own characters. But I am not saying this to shake your faith. Instead, I am trying to show you how completely dependent we are upon His mercy. We must, as St. Augustine has said, be so reduced as to have nothing to present before God but "our wretchedness and His mercy." We are so wretched in our sinfulness that nothing else can ever save us except His mercy. But thank God, His mercy is all we need!

Also, in these times of depression, read whatever will strengthen your confidence and establish your heart. "Truly God is good to Israel, even to such as are of a clean heart" (Psalm 73:1). Let us pray together for this cleanness of heart, which is so pleasing in His sight, and which causes Him to be so compassionate and understanding about our failings.

LETTER 23

Sensitivity to Reproof Is the Surest Sign We Needed It

I certainly want you to have inner peace. But I think you know that this peace does not exist, except for the humble. And there is no real humility unless it is produced by God in every situation. This is especially true in those situations when we are blamed for something by someone who disapproves of us, and when we realize our inner weaknesses. But we might as well get used to both of these trials, for they are tests which we will face again and again.

It is a good sign of real, God-produced humility when we are no longer shocked by the corrections of others, nor by the resistance within. Like little children, we know very well that those correcting us are right, but we also humbly acknowledge the fact that we cannot, by ourselves, make the necessary corrections. We know what we are, and we have no hope of becoming any better except through the mercy of God. The reproofs of others, harsh and unfeeling as they may be, seem to be less than we really deserve. If we find ourselves rebelling and getting irritable, we should understand that this irritability under correction is worse than all our other faults put together. And we know that correction is not going to make us any more humble than it finds us. If we have inner resentment at being corrected that just shows how deeply correction is needed. In fact, the sting of correction wouldn't be felt at all if the old self were dead. So the more correction hurts, the more we see how necessary it is.

I do beg your forgiveness if I have said anything too harsh. But please do not doubt my affection for you. Remember that what I am saying to you does not come from me. It comes from God. And it is the hand of God, which makes use of this awkwardness of mine, to deal a painful blow to that self which causes you so many problems. If I have caused you pain, just remember that the pain proves that I have touched a sore spot. So just yield to God and be content with all His dealings with you, and you will soon have peace and harmony in your soul.

You have often told others about the importance of yielding to God. Now it is important for you to take your own advice. Oh, what wonderful grace will descend upon you if you will accept like a little child all the corrections and reproofs which God uses to humble you and bring you into submission. I pray that he may so completely destroy the self-life in you that it can no longer be found at all.

LETTER 24

Only Imperfection Is Intolerant .of Imperfection

It seems to me that you need to be a little more big-hearted about the imperfection of other people. I know you can't help but see these imperfections when they come right before your eyes and neither can you prevent involuntary opinions about others from popping into your mind. And nobody will deny that the imperfections of others cause us a lot of inconvenience! But it will be enough if you are willing to be patient with imperfections, whether they be serious or not so serious. Do not allow yourself to turn away from people because of their imperfections.

If there is one mark of perfection, it is simply that it can tolerate the imperfections of others. It is able to adjust. It becomes all things to all men. Sometimes we find the most surprising faults in otherwise good people. But we must not be surprised. It is best to let these faults alone and let God deal with them in His time. If *we* deal with them, we shall end up pulling up the wheat with the tares. I have found that God leaves, even in the most spiritual people, certain weaknesses which seem to be entirely out of place. This is true of all of us. And all of us need to be quick to recognize our own imperfection, letting God deal with them.

As for you, labor to be patient with the weaknesses of other people. You know from experience how bitterly it hurts to be corrected. So work hard to make it less bitter for others. Although I am not saying that you correct other people too much. That is not your problem. Your problem is that you became cool when you discover faults in other people, and you tend to quit associating with them. So you need to deal with that problem.

Now, after all that, I ask you more than ever to not spare me if I need correction. Even if you mention a fault which isn't really there, there will be no harm done. If I find that your correction wounds me, then my irritability simply shows that you have touched a sore spot in my life. But if there is no irritability and resentment, then at least you will have done me an excellent kindness in testing my ability to be humble, and in keeping me accustomed to reproof. Since I occupy a position of responsibility in the church, I think I am more responsible to be humble even than others are. God demands that I be dead to everything. I need this, just as you do, and I trust that our mutual need will be the means of cementing, rather than weakening, our attachment in the Lord.

51

LETTER 25

We Should Listen to God and Not to Self

I beg you not to listen to self. Self-love whispers in one ear and the love of God in the other. Self-love is always worthless, aggressive, grasping, and impulsive. But the love of God is so different. It is simple, peaceful, and speaks but a few words in a mild and gentle voice. And the moment we decide to start listening to the voice of self screeching its complaints in our ear, we can no longer hear the more modest whisperings of divine love. You can always tell when self is speaking. Self always wants to entertain itself and never feels sufficiently well attended to. It talks of friendship, regard, esteem, and does not wish to hear anything that is not flattering. The love of God, on the other hand, desires that self should be forgotten, that it should be counted as nothing, that God might be all in all. God knows that it is best for us when self is trampled under foot and broken as an idol, in order that He might live within us, and make us after His will.

So let that vain, complaining babbler—self-love—be silenced, that in the stillness of the soul we may listen to God.

LETTER 26

Absolute Trust Is the Shortest Road to God

I have no doubt that God considers you to be one of His friends; otherwise He would not trust you with so many crosses, sufferings and humiliations. Crosses are God's means of drawing souls closer to Himself. And these crosses accomplish His purposes much more rapidly and effectually than all of our personal efforts put together. Crosses destroy self-love at its very root, down in the depths of the human spirit where we can hardly detect it. But God knows where it is lodged, and He attacks it in its greatest strongholds.

If we have strength and faith enough to trust ourselves completely into the hands of God, and follow Him wherever He leads us there will be no need of stretching and straining to reach perfection. But since we are so weak in faith, and always stopping along the way to ask questions, our journey is lengthened and we get behind in spiritual development. So you see how important it is for you to abandon yourself as completely as possible to God, and continue to do so until your last breath. And don't be afraid. He will never leave you.

LETTER 27

The Time of Temptation and Distress Is No Time to Make Decisions

The overflowing distresses you are going through right now are like the rivers of water that run through the streets after a sudden storm. The only thing you can do is wait until the waters drain away. This is a time of great confusion for you, and nothing seems to make any sense. You are imagining things which aren't true at all. But this is the ordinary reaction to great suffering. Even though you have such a keen mind, God is permitting you to be blind to what lies immediately before you, and he is allowing you to think that you see clearly, when actually, you are only having spiritual mirages. Now I know you want to do the will of God and God will certainly be glorified if you are faithful in yielding to His plans; but nothing could be more unwise than the making of important decisions in this time of distress. A state of distress never produces anything which is of God.

So my advice is this: after you have settled down, make your decisions carefully, then begin to carry out the will of God as you see it. I know this time of distress has been hard on you, but begin now to get back to devotion and simplicity and selflessness. You talk with God, and let Him talk with you. Pay no attention to self. When you are in that sort of relationship with God, then you can go ahead and do whatever is on your heart. I know that a submitted spirit of that sort will not permit you to take a wrong step.

I am sure that you can see how dangerous it is to make decisions when we are in the agonies of distress and under the influence of violent temptations. This is one sure way to go astray. You may ask any experienced counselor you wish, and I am sure he will tell you that you should not make any decisions until you have quieted down. And he will tell you that the easiest way to deceive yourself is to trust your hours of decision making in a time of suffering. At such a time as this, your mind is too unsettled to be trusted.

Now, I know that you think that this decision must be made now or never, and you will no doubt think that I am trying to prevent you from doing what ought to be done. But that is the farthest thing from my mind! As far as this decision is concerned, I do not feel it is my responsibility either to grant you permission or try to hinder you. I only want to give you advice that will keep you in a right relationship with God. And I think it is all too clear that you would be making the wrong decision if you acted simply because self has been wounded and placed on the verge of despair. Is it right to make any decision simply to gratify your self-love, when this is not the will of God? Certainly not! So I strongly advise you to wait until you are in a better condition to accept counsel from the Lord. And the only way we can profit from His Counsel is to maintain a willingness to sacrifice anything for His sake, no matter how much it hurts self.

LETTER 28

If You Have Love, You Have Everything

I have thought a great deal, since yesterday, about the matters of which you wrote me, and I have increasing confidence that God will certainly sustain you in this time of suffering. I can certainly understand how difficult it is for you to wait before God and do all the things you used to do, but be as faithful as you can. You know that a sick person must eat to sustain life, even though he does not feel like it. And a person who is in such a time of distress as you, needs to look to God for sustenance, even though he may not feel like doing it. I think it would be helpful if you could take a few moments with your family occasionally and freely share your feelings with them and have Christian fellowship. Do not be overly concerned about your feelings at this point. I am happy to tell you that God is not expecting any particular kind of emotion from you. All He asks is that you remain faithful. And I rather think that a faithfulness unsustained by pleasant emotion is far purer and reliable than one which depends on tender feelings. Faith which is built on emotion is resting on a very changeable foundation.

A little reading and meditation every day is all that God desires. Through this means, He will give you the light and strength for all the sacrifices He requires. Love Him, and I will release you of every other obligation. For everything else will come by love.

Please understand about love. I am not asking from you a love which is tender and emotional. All I ask is that your will should lean towards love, that you should make up your mind to love God, regardless of your feelings. And no matter what corrupt desires you should find in your heart, if you will make a decision to love God more than self and the whole world, He will be pleased.

LETTER 29

Weakness Preferable to Strength, and Practice Better Than Knowledge

I am told, my dear child in the Lord, that you are suffering from sickness. I want you to know that I suffer along with you, for I love you dearly. But I cannot but adore our wonderful Lord who permits you to be tried in this way. And I pray that you will adore Him along with me. We must never forget those days when you were so lively and energetic, and there is no doubt this was hard on your health. And I rather think that the suffering you are going through now is the natural consequence of your high pressured living.

In this time of physical weakness, I pray that you may become more and more aware of your spiritual weakness. Not that I want you to remain weak. For while the Lord ministers healing and strength to your body, I pray that he will also minister strength to your soul, and that weakness will finally be conquered. But you need to understand that you cannot become strong until first you are aware of your weakness. It is amazing how strong we can become when we begin to understand what weaklings we are! It is in weakness that we can admit our mistakes and correct ourselves while confessing them. It is in weakness that our minds are open to enlightment from others. It is in weakness that we are authoritative in nothing, and say the most clear-cut things with simplicity and consideration for others. In weakness we do not object to being criticized and we easily submit to censure. At the same time, we criticize no one without absolute necessity. We give advice only to those who desire it, and even then we speak with love and without being dogmatic. We speak from a desire to help rather than for a desire to create a reputation for wisdom.

I pray God that he may keep you faithful by His grace, and that He who has begun a good work in you will perform it until the day of Jesus Christ (Phillipians 1:6). Yet, we must be patient with ourselves, (but never flattering), unceasingly using every means of overcoming selfish thoughts and the inconsistencies we have within us. In this way we shall become more susceptible to the Holy Spirit's guidance in the practice of the gospel. But we need to let this spiritual work be done in us quietly and peacefully, not as though it could all be accomplished in a single day. Furthermore, we need to maintain a balance between learning and doing. We ought to spend much more time in doing. If we are not careful, we will spend such a large segment of our lives in gaining knowledge that we shall need another lifetime to put our knowledge into practice. We are in danger of evaluating our spiritual maturity on the basis of the amount of knowledge we have acquired.* But the fact is that education, instead of helping self to die, only nourishes the old man by making him proud of his intellectual attainments. So if you want to make some great strides toward spiritual maturity, then do not trust in your own power or your own knowledge. Humility before God and distrust of your old self, with an open simplicity, are fundamental virtues for you.

*This seems to be one of the most common as well as the most serious mistakes which Christian people are liable to make. God is the giver of knowledge and He desires to have us put it into practice. But the moment we get knowledge. we get so carried away with the delight of having it that we forget there is anything else to be done. But the fact is we have very little reason to rejoice until we put our knowledge into operation in life. Jesus says. "Ye see. but do not perceive—ye hear. but do not understand." Food. lying undigested in the stomach. is not only of no service to the body. but. if not removed. will become harmful. It is only when it is assimilated and mingled with the blood and works itself out into our hands. feet and head that it can be said to have done us any good. So to have an understanding of Biblical truth in the intellect is a matter of Thanksgiving. But it will only result in our condemnation if it is not cherished in the heart and acted out in life. Always remember that it is not knowledge of the way that God desires of us. but the practice of it. Not light. but love. For though I understand all mysteries and all knowledge —but have not love— I am nothing (1 Corinthians 13:2). — Editor.

LETTER 30

Beware of the Pride of Reasoning; the True Guide to Knowledge Is Love

Your mind is too much taken up with your circumstances, and this hinders you from understanding the mind of God. Even worse, I find you too much inclined to arguing and reasoning. I am quite afraid of this inclination to too much reasoning because I think it is such a hinderance to the kind of quiet meditation in which God reveals Himself. You must learn to be humble, simple, and sincerely separated from the ways of men. When you are in the presence of God, be quiet, calm, and do not reason with Him. I am giving you this advice because your most influential friends are such dry, reasoning, critical people that they hinder you in your inner life. Even though you may have resolved to not take spiritual advice from them, yet their endless reasonings about unanswerable questions would, ever so imperceptibly, draw you away from God and finally plunge you into the depths of unbelief. I am pointing out this danger because of the reasoning kind of person you were before your conversion. Habits of long standing are easily revived. And the subtle pressures which cause us to revert to our original position are very difficult to detect, because they seem so natural to us. So be very careful of taking up any habits of the past, no matter how innocent they may seem. Distrust them. You might be starting something which will be the end of you.

I haven't had any leisure time for study for four months now. And even though I enjoy study very much, I am very happy to forego it, and not cling to anything, if this is God's will. It may be that during the coming winter I will have some leisure time for my library, but even then I shall enter it cautiously, keeping one foot on the threshold, ready to leave it whenever God suggests that I should. I believe that the mind needs to fast just as well as the body. You know how much I enjoy writing and speaking, but right now I have no desire to write, or speak, or to be spoken about, or to reason, or to persuade anybody. This may seem like a rather dull way of life to some and it is true that I do have my share of problems, but I do manage to get away from it all and have a little recreation at times. I am a blessedly free man, and I try to do each day whatever I feel the Lord is leading me to do. Of course, those who are trying to figure out where I will be and when are sadly mixed up. God bless them! I am not trying to annoy them, but I insist on freedom in the Lord. I would say to them as Abraham said to Lot, "Is not the whole land before thee? If thou wilt take the left hand, I will go to the right." (Gen. 13:9).

Happy is he who is a free man, but only the Son of God can make us really free. He can do it by breaking every fetter. And how does He do that? By that sword that divides husband and wife, father and son, brother and sister. There is not a person in the world who can be allowed to hinder us from doing the will of God. If we allow the world to hinder us, then our professed freedom is only a word. And we will be as easily captured as a bird whose leg is tied to the ground. He might seem to be free. If the string is delicate enough, you might not even see it. And if it is long enough, the bird might be able to do a little flying. But, nevertheless, he is a prisoner. I hope you see what I am trying to say. Because the freedom that I covet for you to enjoy is far more valuable than all you are fearful of losing.

I want you to be faithful, to put into practice that which you know, that you may be entrusted with more. Do not trust your intellect. It has so often misled you! My own intellect has been such a deceiver that I no longer count upon it. Be simple and firm in your simplicity. Remember that "the fashion of this world passeth away" (I Cor.

7:31) and we shall vanish with it if we make ourselves like it. But the Word of God will never
pass away, and neither shall we if we pay attention
to it and put it into practice.

Again I warn you, beware of philosophers
and the world's great educators. They will always
be a snare to you. I know you have good motives,
and you expect to do them some good by your
associations, but I must warn you that they will
do you more harm than you will do them good.
They spend their time talking about trifling matters and never reach the knowledge of the truth.
They have a greedy desire for knowledge which
can never be satisfied. They are like those con-
querors who wreck and destroy the world without
possessing it. For they gain much knowledge,
without any hope of ever putting it all into practice. Solomon knew all about this from personal
experience and testifies to the vanity of gathering
up knowledge.

I'm convinced that everything we do should
be under the guidance of God. We should not
study unless He guides us to study. And if He
is guiding us to study, then let us meditate on our
studies even on the way to the grocery store.
Let's put our whole heart into it. And then, too,
we must study prayerfully. We must not forget
that God is both Truth and Love. We can only

know the Truth in proportion to our love. When we love Truth, we understand it well. If we do not love Love, we do not know Love. He who loves much and remains humble, is the Well-beloved one of the living Truth. He not only knows more than the philosophers know, but he knows more than they desire to know. I pray that you might obtain that knowledge which is reserved for babes and the simple-minded, while it is hid from the wise and prudent (Matthew 11:25).

LETTER 31

The Gifts of God Are Not to Be Rejected Because of the Channel That Brings Them

I am glad you have found a friend to help you in your time of need. God's ways of providing for us are both beautiful and mysterious. He puts what He pleases where He pleases. Naaman could not be healed by all the waters of Syria, and so had to wash in the waters of Israel. It makes no difference how our help comes. The source is the important thing, not the channel. Of course, God always uses the best channels. And, for us, the best channel is that which most exercises our faith, puts to shame our human wisdom, keeps us simple and humble, and reminds us of our dependence upon God. So, regardless of the channel through which your help has come, reach out and accept whatever help God gives, fully aware of your dependence upon the Holy Spirit that moves wherever He wishes. You can't tell from where He comes, or where He is going (John 3:8). God often sends help in mysterious ways, and we are not trying to understand the secrets of God. We only need to be obedient to what He has revealed to us.

Too much reasoning is a great hindrance to the spiritual life. And you know that the educated men of this world are always quenching the promptings of their conscience by reasoning away what they know to be right, just as the wind extinguishes a candle. And after being with such people for a while, you sense that even your own soul has become dry and off center. Be careful about associating with such people. It is very dangerous, especially for you.

Some of these highly educated people appear to enjoy spiritual meditation, but do not be deceived by appearances. It is easy to mistake intellectual ·curiousity for spiritual hunger. You must understand that men driven by intellectual hunger are really in pursuit of some worldly objective. They are driven by strong desire. They are constantly involved in discussions and reasoning, but they know nothing about that inward peace and silence that listens to God. I mention these people because they are more dangerous than others. You are likely to be deceived by their disguises. And I think if you question them carefully, you will find that they are restless, faultfinding, grasping, worldly, harsh, selfish in all their desires, touchy, full of their own thoughts, and impatient with anyone who contradicts them. In a word, they are spiritual busybodies, annoyed at everything, and almost always annoying everybody else.

LETTER 32

Poverty and Deprivation Are Jesus' Way

Every temptation that comes your way proves what you really are. But God, who loves you, will not permit your temptations to exceed your strength. Instead, He will make use of temptation for your spiritual development.

But let me warn you about the desire to always be looking within to see what progress you are making or how strong you are becoming. The hand of God is invisible, and you cannot always see what He is doing, but be assured that He is very efficient in what He does. Almost anything He does, though, is done in secrecy, and this is a good thing. I don't think we would ever die to self if He were always showing us what He is doing within. If we really understood His sanctifying work and the spiritual graces He is bestowing upon us, we might become very proud. But this is not God's way. Instead of letting us know what He is doing, He works in darkness, and through privation, nakedness and death.

What did Jesus say? Did He say, "if anyone will come after me, let him enjoy himself, let him

71

be well dressed, let him be drunk with happiness (as was Peter on the Mount), let him be glad about his spiritual maturity, let him see how perfect he is in me, let him see himself and be confident that he is perfect?" No, He never said any such thing. On the contrary, His words are, "If any man will come after me, let him deny himself, and take up his cross, and follow me" (Matthew 16:24).

So be open to the ministry of Jesus, and allow Him to strip self-love of every adornment, until it stands barren and exposed. Then you may renounce self and receive the robe whitened by the blood of the Lamb, which is the purity of Jesus. And happy is the soul that no longer possesses anything of its own, not even anything borrowed, and that abandons itself to Jesus, desiring no glory but His. A soul, purified in this manner, is like a bride about to be married. How beautiful she is when she lays everything aside, and comes to the marriage alter bringing nothing but herself. And, oh, Holy Bride, how beautiful are you when you come to Jesus with nothing of your own. The Bridegroom will be more than pleased with you when he sees you clothed in His beauty. There will be no limit to His love for you, because you are clothed in His holiness.

I want you to pay close attention to what I have said, and believe it in faith. Perhaps this truth is bitter, and it might even cause you spiritual indigestion! But your spirit will be fed if you accept the truth about death to self, which is the only true life there is. So believe this, and pay no attention to self. The old self is full of tricks and is more subtle than the serpent who deceived Eve. Happy is the soul who refuses to listen to self, and refuses to pamper it, but listens to God instead.

LETTER 33

The Will of God Our Only Treasure

My desire is that you might have an absolutely settled surrender to the Lord Jesus—a surrender which does not size itself up as being "pretty good"—a surrender which is complete, with nothing held back, no matter how dear it might be. If you have such a surrender as this, you will not deceive yourself. But if you have secret reservations, you are not only deceiving yourself, you are leaving yourself open to deception by the devil.

Also, you must determine to be just as humble and simple when you are out in society as you are in your own prayer closet. Never do anything just because it seems logical, or because it's what you like to do. Whatever you do must be done under submission to the Spirit of life and death (I call Him that because He is the spirit of death to self, and life in God.) Be very careful about great enthusiasm, for even this must be under the control of the Holy Spirit. And when you are tempted to doubt, be careful about searching for certainty within. You have no certainty except in God! Be careful also about looking forward to better

74

things. Even if the present is bitter, yet it is enough for us if it is the will of God. His will is our only treasure. If self is sad because of the present circumstances, do not seek to compensate it by the prospect of the future! We deserve to meet with disappointment when we pamper ourselves like this. Let us accept everything God sends in humility of mind, never asking questions, and always dealing sternly with self. Let God do His work in you, and concentrate on living a selfless life in each and every moment, as though each moment was the whole of eternity.

LETTER 34

Surrender Is Not a Heroic Sacrifice, But a Simple Sinking Into the Will of God

Your only assignment, my dear daughter, is to be strong in faith, no matter what your weaknesses. "When I am weak," says Paul, "then am I strong." Strength is made perfect in weakness. We are only strong in the Lord in proportion to the weakness we sense in ourselves. So your weakness will turn out to be your strength if you accept it humbly.

Sometimes we are tempted to believe that weakness and humility are not compatible with the surrendered life. This is because we tend to think of surrender as that great thing we do when we want to show God how much we love Him, and how heroically we are willing to sacrifice everything. But a true surrender to God has nothing to do with such a flattering description as that.

Let me tell you what real surrender is. It is simply resting in the love of God, as a little baby rests in its mother's arms. A perfect surrender must even be willing to quit surrendering, if that is what God wants! We renounce ourselves, and yet, God never lets us know when it is complete. If we knew, it would no longer *be* complete, for there is nothing that bolsters the ego quite so much as knowing that it is fully surrendered!

Surrender consists, not in doing great, heroic deeds about which self can brag, but simply in accepting whatever God sends, and not seeking to change it (unless it is His will for it to be changed). Full surrender is full peace. If we are restless and concerned about things formerly renounced, we have not genuinely surrendered. Surrender is the source of true peace; if we aren't at peace, it is because our surrender is not complete.

LETTER 35

Bearing Dying Takes the Place of Final Death

We Christians must bear our crosses. In my opinion, self is the greatest cross of them all! We cannot get rid of the weight of that cross until we see that there is nothing that can be done about our condition—that we can only tolerate ourselves as we do our neighbor—and surrender ourselves to God. If we surrender and die to self every day of our lives, there won't be much to do on the last day of our lives. The uncertainties of death will cause no fear when our day comes, if we do not allow these uncertainties to be exaggerated by the worries of self-love. Be patient with your own weaknesses, and be willing to accept help from your neighbor. You will find out in the end, that these little daily deaths will completely destroy the pain of our final dying!

LETTER 36

Suffering Belongs to the Living, Not the Dead

Many are deceived into thinking that the death of self is the cause of all the agony they feel. But that which is dead does not agonize. The more finally and completely we die to self, the less pain we experience. Death is only painful to he who resists it. Self always resists death, because of its intense desire to live! The imagination works over-time, exaggerating the terrors of death. The spirit argues endlessly that the life of self is simply the natural thing. Self-love fights against death, like a sick man in his last struggle. But regardless of the protests of self, we must die inwardly as well as outwardly. The sentence of death has gone forth against the Spirit as well as against the body. The body must die because of sin. But the spirit must die *to* sin, and to itself. Be sure that your spirit dies first (to itself), and then our bodily death will be as peaceful as falling asleep. Happy are they who sleep this sleep of peace!

LETTER 37

God Gives Grace in Proportion to Our Trials

I feel a deep sense of sympathy for your loved one who is suffering so much. And I can certainly appreciate the concern of those God-given friends who are trying to help her bear her cross. Tell her not to lose faith in God. The grace He gives will be in direct proportion to the amount of suffering she must bear. No one else can do this except the Creator who made us and knows how to renew our strength by His grace. None of us are wise enough to properly apportion grace and suffering. We cannot see the extent of our future trials, nor of the vast supplies of which God is storing up in us so that we can meet them. And because we cannot see those future trials, nor the grace that will be needed for them, we are tempted to become discouraged and despondent in our present situations. We see our trials rolling in toward us like great, overpowering, ocean waves. Our hearts fail us with fear at the prospect of drowning. We do not see that we stand within the point at which God, with a steady finger, has drawn the boundary line. Beyond that line the waves cannot pass.

God often allows us to be tested as one is tested by a stormy sea. God stirs up the sea, and makes its great billows seem to threaten destruction. But He is always at hand to say, "Thus far shalt thou go and no farther."

"God is faithful, Who will not suffer you to be tempted above that ye are able to bear it" (I Cor. 10:13).

LETTER 38

Resisting God, an Effective Hindrance to Grace

Down deep in your heart I believe you know what God demands of you, but you are resisting Him. And this is the cause of all your distress. You are beginning to think that it is impossible for you to do what God requires. But recognize this for what it is: a temptation to give up hope. Now it's quite all right for you to give up hope about self (it will never be any better!), but never give up hope in God. He is all good and all powerful, and He will give whatever you need according to your faith. If you will believe all things, all things shall be yours, and you shall even remove mountains. But if you believe nothing, you shall have nothing. And only you will be to blame. Look at Abraham, who hoped against every reasonable hope! Look at Mary, who, when the most incredible thing in the world was proposed to her, did not hesitate, but exclaimed, "be it unto me according to thy word" (Luke 1:38).

So open up your heart to the riches of God's grace. You are now so locked up within yourself that you not only do not have the power to do what is required of you, but you do not even desire to have it. You actually seem to be afraid of what might happen if you open up to God's grace in this situation. And, of course, God's grace cannot fill your heart when it is so completely locked up.

All I ask of you is that you have a teachable spirit of faith, and do not pay any attention to self. Simply trust everything into the hands of God, be humble, and open up to His grace. Through meditation and prayer, you will receive peace, and everything will gradually be worked out for you. And the things which, in your hour of temptation, seemed so difficult will disappear almost imperceptibly.

LETTER 39

God Speaks More Effectually in the Soul Than to It

Nothing gives me more satisfaction to see you living so simply and peacefully. Simplicity brings back the joys of Paradise. Not that we have pure pleasure without a moment's suffering, but when we are surrendered to God, we are not grasping for pleasure, and even our troubles are received with thanksgiving. This inner harmony, and this deliverance from fear and the tormenting desires of self, create a satisfaction in the soul which is above all the intoxicating joys of this world put together. So be content to live, then, in the earthly paradise which God has prepared for you, and be careful not to leave it to satisfy the vain desire of knowing good and evil.

Do not give in to self pity when God permits you to be alone. We are never less alone than when we are in the company of a single friend. And God is that friend. We are never less deserted than when we are carried in His everlasting arms. Nothing is more touching than to know that God hurries to help us. And when God sends help through one of His servants, the value of that help is not affected in any way by the servant, no matter how foul and spiritually barren that servant may be. The help comes from God, and it is good. Now if God were to put a veritable fountain of His grace in your heart, there would be no need of any channels to bring His grace to you. And this is exactly what God has done. "God, who at sundry times and in divers manners spake in time past unto the fathers by the prophets, hath in these last days spoken unto us by His Son" (Hebrews 1:1-2). The Son of God, living within the soul is that fountain of grace. Shall we then feel any regret that the feeble voice of the old prophets has ceased? What useless regret! How pure and powerful is the voice of God when He speaks within the soul! And He always does this whenever other channels of grace are cut off.

LETTER 40

The Circumcision of the Heart

Our eagerness to serve others often arises from mere natural generosity instead of a real Christian love. Sometimes, serving others seems like a good way for self to convince itself of how good it really is. But service which does not come out of real love will soon turn sour. True love is simple and always the same toward its neighbor. It is humble, and never thinks of itself. Anything which is incompatible with divine love must be renounced.

It is by the circumcision of the heart (the cutting away of selfish impurity) that we are made children of Abraham's family of faith. And, like Abraham, we are able to leave our native country without knowing where we are going. What a blessed lot in life! To leave all and yield ourselves to the cutting of God's knife of circumcision. Who could do the job of cutting away sin better than He? Our own hands would never put the knife in the right place. We would cut away only a little of the fat, and bring about a few superficial changes. We do not understand ourselves well enough to know where to cut. We could never find the sensitive spot, but God finds it easily. And even if we knew where the spot were located, self-love would hold back the knife and spare itself. It does not have the courage to wound itself. And even if the knife were plunged into the vital spot, the nerves would steel themselves against the pain, and the teeth would be gritted, in order to deaden some of the pain. But the hand of God strikes in unexpected places, finds the very place where the infection is fastened and does not hesitate to cut it away, regardless of the pain. And oh, how self-love cries out! Well, let it cry, but do not let it interfere with the success of the operation. God knows that it hurts, but all that He asks is that you remain motionless beneath his knife and do not resist a single stroke.

I have a great liking for John the Baptist, who completely forgot himself so that he might think only of Jesus. He pointed to Him. He was the voice of one crying in the wilderness to prepare His way. He sent all of his disciples to Him. And it was this willingness to magnify Jesus, far more than his solitary and strict life, that entitled him to be called the greatest among them that are born of women.

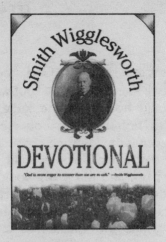

Smith Wigglesworth Devotional
Smith Wigglesworth

You are invited to journey with Smith Wigglesworth
on a year-long trip that will quench your spiritual
thirst while it radically transforms your faith.
As you daily explore these challenging insights
from the Apostle of Faith, you will connect with
God's glorious power, cast out doubt, and see
impossibilities turn into realities. Your prayer life
will never be the same again when you personally
experience the joy of seeing awesome, powerful
results as you extend God's healing grace to others.

ISBN: 0-88368-574-4 • Trade • 560 pages

www.whitakerhouse.com